The Location of Heaven in the Universe

The Location of *Heaven* in the Universe

Richard LeRoy Clements

XULON PRESS

Xulon Press
2301 Lucien Way #415
Maitland, FL 32751
407.339.4217
www.xulonpress.com

© 2023 by Richard LeRoy Clements

All rights reserved solely by the author. The author guarantees all contents are original and do not infringe upon the legal rights of any other person or work. No part of this book may be reproduced in any form without the permission of the author.

Due to the changing nature of the Internet, if there are any web addresses, links, or URLs included in this manuscript, these may have been altered and may no longer be accessible. The views and opinions shared in this book belong solely to the author and do not necessarily reflect those of the publisher. The publisher therefore disclaims responsibility for the views or opinions expressed within the work.

Unless otherwise indicated, Scripture quotations taken from the King James Version (KJV) – *public domain.*

Scripture taken from The Passion Translation (TPT). Copyright © 2017 by Passion & Fire Ministries, Inc. Used by permission. All rights reserved. thePassionTranslation.com

Paperback ISBN-13: 978-1-66287-691-2
Ebook ISBN-13: 978-1-66287-692-9

Table of Contents

Introduction: Hearing God's Voice 1

Fiery Trials: God's Prescence in the Chaos........... 7

Strive to Seek God for Strength 13

Humble Yourself; Listen for God's Voice 17

Setting the Stage 23

A Mother's and Father's Love in One............... 29

God's Revelation of Love 35

The Light of God's Radiant Glory 41

Conclusion: God is in the Sunshine 57

About the Author................................ 61

References..................................... 63

Introduction: Hearing God's Voice

The year was 2008, the year of the crash and the beginning of the Great Recession. I was sitting in my study when I heard the Holy Spirit speak to me. What He said was very clear. Before I reveal what He said to me, I would like to share a bit about myself to further prove to you that I know His voice and heard it while I was going through the worst time of my life.

I was part owner of a construction debris hauling business with my twin brother, Steve, and our lifelong friend, Tom. We serviced most of the suburbs in the growth hub of Chicago during the building boom from the mid-1990s to 2008. We specialized in new construction debris removal. God had led us to start our own business.

Before this endeavor, we had all worked with my dad's business pouring concrete for about ten years. My wonderful wife, Donna, and I got married very young, and my brother started dating Donna's sister, Dawn, right after our wedding. Their father, Chester, was a very hard-working Polish man from a Polish neighborhood on the North Side of Chicago. He worked for a major snack company delivering their products to the stores in the suburbs. He brought home a weekly check, so our wives were accustomed to life with a steady income.

Construction was the opposite of that. The construction economy in Chicago was like a roller coaster between the recessions, bad weather, and union strikes. Life was a struggle, and it was very hard on our wives. Our partner's wife, Barb, grew up in an electrician's home, so she was used to the uncertainties in income.

Donna, like her dad, worked very hard, and as soon as the kids were all in school, she went to school to become a nurse. She worked hard and really helped our family enjoy a better life. When the economy crashed in 2008 and we went into the great recession, our family survived because God had positioned Donna in a stable position. She worked hard to be a great nurse, and she was. Dawn and Barb had to work hard for their families, as well. At the time, God moved the three of us to go into business. Our wives had been enjoying a steady income for a few years, so they weren't too excited to hear about our plan.

In those days, the waste industry was a land of giants, so it was a huge step of faith for us. We found ourselves trusting God daily because we really needed Him. We were learning that God designs our lives according to His purposes, like when He chose Mary and Joseph to raise His Son. He didn't choose a financially successful couple; He chose a carpenter and a young woman who would be dependent upon Him daily.

We were certain God was calling us to start our business, but felt highly unqualified. We had not gone to college because we were raised by a couple who were also dependent on God daily. Both of our parents were descendants of our nation's founding fathers. Their ancestors came to America in the mid-1600s–talk about depending on God daily!

Our parents raised nine children on a concrete contracting business in the northern suburbs of Chicago. Winters in Chicago were often too cold to pour concrete, so they never had an abundance of money. The three of us had instant jobs every summer with my dad's business and could make pretty good money, so none of us saw the value of going to college. Since my dad needed laborers, he didn't push us to go to college, either. Looking back now, at the age of sixty-five, I can see it was all part of God's plan. He was setting the stage for us to depend on Him.

I found that when you are dependent on the Father, He will strengthen your faith by bringing you to impossible and uncomfortable circumstances, and just when you think He isn't going to come through, He does! I discovered that after you've been through those circumstances a few hundred times, you learn you can trust Him more. The secret to learning to trust Him sooner is to praise Him and thank Him before breakthrough comes. It's easy to praise Him after He comes through, but we tend to forget quickly what He did. He wants us to trust Him because He loves us, and the best way to trust God is to get to know Him.

The hard things that God allows to come into your life's journey are intended to draw you closer to Him, but until you know the depth of His love, or taste of His love, it's hard to trust Him. Hard things will surely come into every life, so it is imperative that you get to know the Father as soon as possible.

The way to get to know the Father is to spend time talking and listening to Him. It is best to make a place where you can be alone with Him every morning or evening. You need a prayer closet. It can be a room, a garden, or a literal closet. If you go in and meet with Him, He will show up. It helps to have soft Christian music or "soaking" music to quiet your mind so you can hear His still, small voice.

Over the course of this book, it is my hope to share how God helped me through my difficult circumstances, share how He can help you through yours, and where I believe heaven may be found. I also hope to encourage you the same way God used this revelation to encourage me.

Fiery Trials: God's Prescence in the Chaos

My dad, Aaron LeRoy Clements, went through a fire when he was thrust into World War II in 1945. Since he was in the National Guard at the beginning of the war, his unit was sent in after the losses of D-Day. They brought the unit into the Army, and they arrived just as the U.S. and other allied armies were crossing the Rhine to attack Germany. The resistance was very strong, and he was in the very front lines of one of the invading armies. He was a medic, as well as a liberator, so he saw a lot of dead and wounded men.

He was in a small scout platoon that they sent ahead to look for the concentration camps. He was the first soldier to enter the Kaufering concentration camp, which was the closest subcamp of Dachau. Since he was a liberator, what he saw in the camp was much worse than what he had seen on the battlefield.

At that time, his unit had a very high casualty rate. They would try to rotate the soldiers on the front lines after a couple of weeks, so the soldiers could get rest. Frequently, when they tried to take my dad off duty, his replacement would get killed or badly wounded. So, before he could even get into the shower, they put him back on duty.

Then, my father endured a fiery trial that made what he was going through much worse. The prisoners they were capturing became a problem. As you can imagine, supplies were short, and his commanding officers gave orders to shoot the prisoners because the Germans started killing the American prisoners. My dad stood against them because the medics were responsible to take care of wounded soldiers on both sides, if possible.

The commanding officers decided my dad must have been a German sympathizer and set up a kangaroo court to try him. During the trial, they said my dad probably never lost a loved one in the war. However, that very day, he had received a letter from his mother informing him that his older brother had been killed in the Battle of the Bulge. He took it out of his pocket and threw it on the table, and they backed off. God used my dad to save the lives of those same men who were accusing him later down the road. This was similar to the situation Desmond Dawes experienced, who later became famous for the historic night when he heroically saved seventy-five men in the Battle of Hacksaw Ridge.

God was close to my dad in the war because he was seeking Him the whole time he was overseas. Men got shot right next to him many times. He had a round hit his jacket collar once, and one hit his helmet, but it did not penetrate. That "fire" of war strengthened his faith and he saw that God was faithful, since the bullets never got him.

A similar example of a fiery trial that moved hearts to seek the Lord is that of the Israelites going through their journey to the promised land. Along the way, God instructed them to build the ark of the covenant to contain His presence so He could travel with them as He moved them.

> *And they shall make an ark of shittim wood: two cubits and a half shall be the length thereof, and a cubit and a half the breadth thereof, and a cubit and a half the height thereof. And thou shalt overlay it with pure gold, within and without shalt thou overlay it, and shalt make upon it a gold crown, round about.* Exodus 25:10-11

The way this ark was designed by God was a model of our walk with God (when we choose to strive to enter the strait gate as mentioned in Luke 13:24). It's also a model of the journey God's people were on to get to the promised land. That journey is a model for us on our own spiritual journey with the Lord as He leads us into intimacy with Him.

God intended that the Israelites' journey into the wilderness would be difficult in order to show them that He was real, and that He would be their God.

When God tested them, He would eliminate something important like food or drink, and they became fearful. The Israelites would then murmur and complain instead of trusting God. God would meet their needs, but they soon forgot, and found themselves in the next test. We all do this in our journey with the Lord. Same test, different need.

When they finally got near to the entrance to the promised land, they had to camp in the Shittim Forest. It must have been a real "shittim" place; a thorn tree forest, the wood from which they made the ark of the covenant. This wood is called acacia wood now, and it is the main layer of material that contains the Father's presence. Thorn trees are very hard to cut or break. Much striving is required to live in a thorn tree forest. So, the question remains, "Lord, will only a few have eternal life?"

Strive to Seek God for Strength

Strive to enter in at the strait gate: for many, I say unto you, will seek to enter in, and shall not be able. Luke 13:24

The devil, your stomach your pets, your loved ones, and a thousand things will all come against the time you set apart for prayer since it is the most vital time of your life.

The word "strive" in Greek means to struggle; compete for a prize (literally); to contend with an adversary (figuratively).

The word "seek" means in Hebrew to worship God, or in Greek to seek, search after, look for, to inquire into, examine, consider, to strive for, desire or wish. (Strong's Concordance)

Seeking alone isn't enough. That's why God says, "If you seek Me with your whole heart, you will find Me" (Jeremiah 29:13). In the same way, no one wins a championship in sports by just seeking it. An athlete must strive for it, and it requires a great coach to motivate them to whole-hearted performance.

> *For as the heavens are higher than the earth, so are My ways higher than your ways, and My thoughts than your thoughts.* Isaiah 55:9

God's ways are different from ours. He will be hard on you because like a good coach, He will push you into hardship. Hardship strengthens you for the future. When He wanted to make Israel a great people, He put them into hard labor. They became slaves to the Egyptians.

God strengthened the people of color the same way. They have great athletic ability today because of the strength of their ancestors, which had gotten them through hard work as slaves. God was setting them free, and freedom requires strength, especially inner strength, that comes through trials in life.

I love America because of the diversity of all of the different people who have come here. Their giftings are incredible! I loved the music diversity of the 50s and early 60s. Motown was awesome, as well as American, English, and Irish music. Those were great times for about ten or fifteen years, but we slid away from God through drugs, alcohol, and everything else that felt good. Today, God wants to bless our nation; however, He knows we need to be strengthened through fiery trials in preparation for the coming prosperity. He keeps calling His people to come up to higher places of His presence. It seems, though, that once we experience a little comfort, we just want to sit down and relax.

We must strive to enter a consistent prayer life. This requires us to quiet our flesh and mind so God can speak to us. We need God's strategy to strive. It's not by the sweat of our brow, but by His Spirit. King David knew this strategy because when he was a young shepherd, God had him in just the right place to use his musical talents to quiet the mind of King Saul. God had sent an evil spirit to trouble Saul, and rejected Saul as king because of his disobedience.

> *It is a good thing to give thanks unto the Lord, and to sing praises unto Thy name O, Most High; to shew forth thy lovingkindness in the morning, and thy faithfulness every night. Upon an instrument of ten strings, and upon the psaltery; Upon the harp with a solemn sound.* Psalms 92:1-3

Today, we have a style of music called "soaking" music (as I mentioned earlier) that is for the sole purpose of relaxing your mind and heart. If you are curious, YouTube has some great selections you can try out.

Humble Yourself;
Listen for God's Voice

When God does a new thing, He needs people who are humble. Most people do not handle change very well since they like to follow what has worked in the past. That is why, many times, a fiery trial is required.

As I had shared before, Tom, Steve, and I went through a season of developing a whole new system of debris removal in the construction industry. This system took several years of struggling to develop, and just happened to be the perfect system for the national home builders during the housing boom around Chicago that peaked from 2000 to 2007. God never showed us a blueprint to follow. We were on a "need-to-know" basis as He developed it. He would bring us to a place of need, and then show us His provision for that need. Everything happened from following the Holy Spirit's lead one day at a time, line upon line. He kept us dependent upon Him, and everything came out of a need to survive. God would reveal things to us when we needed to come up with a solution to meet our customer's changing needs.

The reason I'm sharing briefly about our business is so you can understand that my partners and I could hear God's voice. It was no coincidence our system was the perfect system for our customers. Neither the home builders nor my partners and I even knew they would need a different system. Sales were good, and the builders were moving at a fast pace, building ten houses a week in their projects. Consequently, that became the most menial part of the whole construction operation. The garbage, on the other hand, quickly became the biggest problem.

Building a house requires a lot of activity, and the conventional roll-off dumpster was too big and always in the way. They had schedules planned out. Oftentimes, a worker would come to the site to do something on a house, the big dumpster would be in the way, and it would hinder their schedule. God helped us to develop a collection truck and system that would alleviate problems when production was accelerated. Our new bin was small enough that they could move it if it was in the way.

One of the home builders had a young project manager named Mike, who was a great leader and wasn't afraid to try new ideas. Using our new system was a big risk for him because the big companies were often very competitive among the employees. He gave our system a chance and it worked great.

We did not come up with this idea; it was all God's plan. God is so wise in the way He does things. He keeps us on a "need-to-know" basis because we would think His way was incomprehensible if He showed us in advance. While developing that system, I thought we were crazy! I'm sure our competitors thought we were crazy, as well, but God's way is always the best way at the perfect time. God knows the future, so He will set you up for it if you give Him your life and walk with Him through life's journey.

This book is not about the business God gave us, but about a God who loves us very much, and wants to walk with us in life. He wants us to get to know Him and experience His great love for us. He is no respecter of persons, and He will do awesome things through anyone who draws near to Him. When you look back over the years of your journey, you will see you were not remiss, but rather exactly where you were supposed to be.

When you ask Jesus into your life, His life is born into you, and you are called a born-again Christian. Jesus will grow in your life, and just like your physical life, your spiritual life will grow over time. You see, things in the natural realm demonstrate what happens in the spiritual realm. When I bought the property, it was a vacant lot. Donna and I planted seven pine trees and many bushes. Over the years, they grew slowly, but surely. Now, the pine trees grew to fifty feet tall and the bushes are ten feet tall.

Jesus said His kingdom would grow in your life the same way. He used the illustration of the mustard seed in the Book of Matthew.

> *Then Jesus taught them another parable: Heaven's kingdom can be compared to the tiny mustard seed that a man takes and plants in his field. Although the smallest of all the seeds, it eventually grows in to the greatest of garden plants, becoming a tree for the birds to come and build their nests in its branches.*
> Matthew 13:31-32 (TPT)

When you let Jesus into your life, He can become the biggest part of your life. He will fill you with His Holy Spirit if you let Him. The Holy Spirit is awesome; He will lead you into all truth. He doesn't come in and take over your life. He only takes what you give Him. He is a great leader to help you through life.

Setting the Stage

I know you bought this book to find out where heaven is in the universe, and I will show you in Scripture how the Holy Spirit showed me. First, I must set the stage for you. I've written briefly about how my brother, our best friend, and I were led to start a construction debris removal business. This call took us all out of our fathers' construction companies and into the waste hauling business. Our business grew into a multi-million dollar company for the last couple of years before the crash. We thought we were on our way to the great purpose God had promised us. Then the crash in 2008 happened.

Looking back through the years and reading God's Word, it became clear to us that God had done this before. The story of Joseph, found in Genesis chapters 39 through 50, stood out to me. This is one of the greatest stories in the Bible. It is a true story of how God had chosen a young boy to reveal Himself and His plan through dreams, and how God gave him the gift of interpreting dreams. It was a gift that would make him second-in-command of the greatest country on Earth at that time. I would encourage you to read this story from your Bible, but allow me to paraphrase it for you.

Joseph had gotten a job with Potiphar, who was an officer and chief executioner of the royal guard. He was working in the administration, and he had favor with his boss because of the gifting he had from God. It appeared to him that he was on his way to the top, as his dreams had indicated. Suddenly, he was falsely accused and thrown into prison. This was the complete opposite place to which he felt God was taking him and he was there for a long time, until God made a way for him.

His gift became urgently needed. Pharaoh, the top dog of Egypt, had a troubling dream, and he told it to all of his wise men and magicians, but no one could interpret the dream. Joseph, who just happened to be imprisoned with a couple of the Pharaoh's servants two years earlier, both had troubling dreams. Joseph was able to interpret them because he had that gift from God. One of the servants remembered Joseph and told Pharaoh how Joseph had interpreted his dream. Immediately, Pharaoh sent for him. When Joseph came before Pharaoh, he was careful to let him know it was God who gave him the talent needed to interpret his dream. Pharaoh was so impressed with Joseph that he appointed him as governor to the whole land of Egypt.

My point of sharing this story is to show you God's ways are strange to us. We must be flexible and trust the Father all the time. His ways are higher than our ways. He has reasons for doing things that we do not understand, but when you really get to know Him, you just know He wants the best for you.

This is what I heard clearly in my heart that day in 2008.

I was sitting quietly in my study in a state of total despondency. I had three fires raging in my life at that time. Our business was in a nosedive because of the 2008 crash, my mother was passing away, and Donna and I were having relational problems. Then, I heard the Holy Spirit say very clearly in my heart, "Ya *know, heaven is inside the sun.*"

Just like that, He said it! But my reaction in my despondency was like, "That is ridiculous, and people will think I am crazy if I share it with anyone."

I was not even thinking about where heaven was at that time. It was the furthest thing from my mind. Then, He started revealing things to me that proved His word to me. A couple of days later, I was reading something on my computer, and I saw a side article about the sun that said, "NASA scientists have always known that the center of the sun is cooler than the corona of the sun, and they didn't know why." This caught my attention.

Then I started searching for more information on the sun. The corona is the outermost layer of the sun's atmosphere. The size of the sun is so big that one million Earths could fit inside its sphere. That is a huge amount of space, and there is no way for scientists to film past the surface of the corona. Therefore, it is a mystery what is inside the sun. They're still trying to figure out what is inside the earth. The Bible says that hell is beneath and is referred to as the lake of fire (Revelation 20:15), and every time there is a volcanic eruption, it seems to confirm that hell is real. The Bible can show us things that the greatest minds in the world haven't even figured out yet.

The Father has revealed to me many scriptural proofs and a few more scientific proofs, as well, that I will share throughout the remaining pages of this book.

> *In my distress I called upon the Lord and cried unto my God: He heard my voice out of His temple, and my cry came before Him, even into His ears. Then the earth shook and trembled; the foundations also of the hills moved and were shaken, because He was wroth. There went up a smoke out of His nostrils, and fire out of His mouth devoured: Coals were kindled by it. He bowed the heavens also and came down: and the darkness was under*

His feet. And He rode upon a cherub, and did fly: Yea, He did fly upon the wings of the wind. He made darkness His secret place; His pavilion round about Him were dark waters and thick clouds of the skies. At the brightness that was before Him his thick clouds passed, hail stones and coals of fire. The Lord also thundered in the heavens, and The Highest gave His voice; hail stones and coals of fire.
Psalms 18:6-13

Another time that God the Father came down was in Exodus chapter 24. He came to talk to Moses on Mt. Sinai.

And Moses went up into the mount, and a cloud covered the mount. And the glory of the Lord abode upon mount Sinai, and the cloud covered it for six days: and the seventh day He called unto Moses out of the midst of the cloud. And the sight of the glory of the Lord was like devouring fire on top of the mount un the eyes of the children of Israel. And Moses went into the midst of the cloud, and gat him up into the mount: and Moses was in the mount forty days and forty nights.
Exodus 24:15-18 (KJV)

When Moses came down from Mt. Sinai with the two tablets of the testimony in his hands, he did not know that the skin on his face shown and sent forth beams by reason of speaking with the Lord. When Aaron and all of the Israelites saw Moses's face, they feared to come near him. This radiant "glory of God" is an amazing thing. It is part of the Father's environment. The glory of the Lord is so bright that He had to hide Himself in a dark cloud.

The word "glory" is very interesting. Glory has two opposite meanings, like two sides of a coin. Consider the brilliance of the sun. It makes everything beautiful and brings us comfort and warmth, yet the opposite effects of the sun cause aging, damage, and drought. So it was with the Father's revelation of Himself. In the Old Testament, He first revealed His glory to His chosen vessels in great and terrifying ways, yet in the New Testament, He revealed His glory as love, mercy, and grace through His Son, Jesus Christ.

One meaning of glory is "kavod," which means glory, honor, distinction, weighty, or heavy. The other is "shekhina" which means to reside or permanently stay; the act of dwelling; fire; the manifestation of God's presence. It's like a double-edged sword. You can either be under the heavy hand of the Father and life can be very hard, or you can be in the Father's graces and things go from blessing to blessing.

A Mother's and Father's Love in One

Many of His children have been on both sides of the Father's hand. His desire is that we would totally surrender to His will and come into His intimate love. A problem occurs when our carnal nature responds to the Father's blessings, and we become prideful. Because of this, our love for the Father tends to cool, and we focus on His blessings rather than His presence.

He knows that we are headed for trials and hardship when we begin to lose our first love, so He uses life's difficulties, hoping to bring us into the intimate revelation of His love, which in Job's case was the ultimate outcome in the story. The coolest thing about all of this is the Father wants more than anything for us to experience His peace and presence, and to show us He is everything we are searching for in this life.

Men, our Father is a mother's love that you may be trying to find in a woman. Women, He is a father's love you may be looking for in a man. You may be hoping to make your wife or your husband house that love and respect that you are seeking, but they are unable to provide what only the Father can give. So, we ultimately have conflict and confrontations with our spouses, and oftentimes will find ourselves turning to someone else, only to go through the same struggles all over again. If you find yourself in this scenario, I suggest bowing to the Father and asking Him to help you draw near to Him. He will satisfy all your longings.

Religion is man's attempt to earn God's favor, but it puts you in the heavy yoke. The coolest thing is that you already have God's favor and He wants you to join Jesus, Who has the easy yoke (Matthew 11:28-30). Jesus is yoked to the Father, and the Father does the heavy lifting. He isn't concerned about our accomplishments; He just wants us to want Him. Very few people know the unconditional love of the Father in this way.

This is what the great last day revival or latter-day harvest is all about. People will experience the revelation of the Father's love that Jesus taught and manifested the entire time He was on Earth.

I think a good picture of the way Jesus revealed the Love of the Father was in the movie *The Wizard of Oz*. Oz was the terrifying voice that kept everyone in fear and controlled them to follow rules that were established. Toto, Dorothy's dog, went to the secret hiding place where the voice was coming from and pulled back the curtain to reveal a very sweet, older man who provided the answer for each of the characters who came to him for their needs.

There is a story in the Old Testament that demonstrates the way the people feared God. God called His people out to Mt. Sinai to talk to them.

> *And the Lord said unto Moses, Lo, I come unto thee in a thick cloud, that the people may hear when I speak with thee and believe thee forever. And Moses told the words of the people to the Lord. And the Lord said unto Moses, Go unto the people, and sanctify them today and tomorrow, and let them wash their clothes, and be ready against the third day, for the third day: the Lord will come down in the sight of all the people upon Mt. Sinai. And thou shall set bounds unto the people round about, saying, Take heed to yourselves, that ye go not up into the mount, or touch the border of it: whosoever toucheth the mount shall surely be put to death: there shall not a hand touch it, but he shall surely be stoned or shot through; whether it be beast or man, it shall not live: when the trumpet soundeth long, they shall come up to the mount.* Exodus 19:9-13

Once sin was atoned for when Jesus died on the cross, the Father wanted to reveal His loving nature to His people. At the crucifixion, the Father comes down and the scene is described very similarly to when He came down on Mt. Sinai.

> *Now from the sixth hour there was darkness over all the land unto the ninth hour... Jesus, when he had cried again with a loud voice, yielded up the ghost. And, behold, the veil of the temple was rent in twain from the top to the bottom; and the earth did quake, and the rocks rent;* Matthew 27:45, 50-51

Now, the Word specifically says the curtain ripped from the top to the bottom. That's very significant. The Father tore it. This revealed that now people could go directly into the Father's presence. The whole reason God created man was for fellowship. The Father's long-awaited moment had come. We don't have to come to God through a religion or a priest. We can freely come to Him in the name of Jesus once we receive Jesus as our Savior. Jesus's Father becomes our Father, and all Christians become our brothers and sisters. God's kingdom is a family kingdom. Jesus made a big deal of this after He rose from the dead. When Mary came to the sepulcher and was looking for His body, Jesus appeared to her.

> *Jesus cautioned her, "Mary, don't cling to me, for I haven't yet ascended to God, my Father. And He's not only my Father and God, but now he's your Father and your God! Now go to my brothers and tell them what I've told you, that I am ascending to my Father— and your Father, and to my God— and your God!"* John 20:17 (TPT)

Now, that is a big deal! God has now become our Father when we accept Jesus as our Savior. His love is so powerful that He can love each one of us as if we were the only son or daughter in the universe. He knows everything about us, including how many hairs are on our heads, and this number changes every day. He told us this in order that we could see Him as our wonderful Father. Jesus revealed the Father's feminine nature, as well. The closest example we have of the Father's love is a wonderful mother's love.

> *As one whom his mother comforteth, so will I comfort you; and ye shall be comforted in Jerusalem.* Isaiah 66:13

God's Revelation of Love

John 17 is a great chapter of the New Testament that reveals the growth process of the believer (I highly recommend reading The Passion Translation as it is a beautiful version of this chapter). Starting on verse 6, Jesus prays for His disciples. The prayer begins with Jesus telling the Father how He revealed Him to the men and women that the Father had given to Him, and how they had "fastened" His word to their hearts. So, they had believed in Jesus, and had His word in their hearts. These are the first two stages of growth for a believer.

Next, He states that eternal life means to know and experience the Father as the only true God, and to know and experience Jesus Christ as the one and only Son He sent. Many people know about God the Father and Jesus His Son; however, these ones may have not yet experienced Them. It is quite possible to miss the greatest thing in heaven and on Earth, which is the loving presence of God. Since knowing the Father and His Son is eternal life, you can have Him now. You don't have to wait until you pass away.

Jesus then prays for His disciples for something they had not yet fully attained. Verse 13 states, *But now I am returning to you, Father, and I pray that they will experience and enter into My joyous delight in You so that it is fulfilled in them and overflows.* This is the "love of the Father" which He is revealing to our generation right now. It took me thirty-eight years to enter into this "joyous delight" and it is the most awesome place I have ever been. I believe in these last days people will encounter and experience the Father's love as they come to Christ.

You can have a relationship with Him and have true love, peace, and joy rather than the counterfeit feelings that come from alcohol or drugs. The "peace" found in alcohol and drug is fake and expensive. Jesus's peace is real and it's free. One of the reasons that Jesus taught the "Our Father" prayer to His disciples was to show them that He wanted His followers to daily experience the faithfulness of the Father. He promises to meet all our needs, and always does. He will never let you down.

Like Jesus serving the best wine at the later part of the wedding feast, the Father is revealing the best part of Himself at the end of the age. We are entering the latter harvest, as the Word of God mentions. God is bringing many people into His kingdom by a huge harvest of souls.

Love comes from God because God is love. Jesus called the natural disasters "birth pangs." In our day, we can that these things are increasing in intensity, aand are coming ,closer together to birth the kingdom of God back into this earth. (IIW)

Worship music draws people to God. When we worship God, we experience His loving presence which is peace and security. What a great time to be alive! Father God is revealing His awesome compassion for those who are becoming His children. We are being taken into the depths of God's love.

The Pharisee Saul, who was a very ambitious religious leader, was caught up in the pride of life and was trying so hard to be a great religious leader. He was killing the new Christian church that God was establishing on Earth, but God got a hold of him one day. He knocked him off his high horse and struck him blind so He could help him to see spiritual things. Saul was soon renamed Paul and chosen and commissioned by God to bring the good news of salvation through Jesus Christ to the world. Paul was used to reveal more about the love of the Father than any other human. The living Christ in Paul revealed the way to the Father's love throughout the remainder of Paul's life.

Isn't it amazing that the Almighty God of the universe is a loving Father to the people who will choose to be in His family? We get to be in the family of the God Who created and owns everything in the universe.

God expresses His love this way:

> *That he would grant you, according to the riches of his glory, to be strengthened with might by his Spirit in the inner man; that Christ may dwell in your hearts by faith; that ye, being rooted and grounded in love, may be able to comprehend with all saints what is the breadth, and length, and depth, and height; and to know the love of Christ, which passeth knowledge that ye might be filled with all the fulness of God.* Ephesians 3:16-19

God is speaking of knowing the love of Christ from the experience of spending time with Him, not by simply hearing and learning about it. He is so real! If you believe, take time out of your day, and go to a quiet place to talk to Him, He will come near and fill you. Then, His Holy Spirit will fill you up with His love. He will have a relationship with you as though you are the only one in the universe. His love is that awesome. The love of God is the thing we need the most. Life makes no sense without it.

The reason I am highlighting the love of the Father is so you will understand that a Father Who loves the people He created this much, would not separate Himself to the other end of the universe, or any another dimension. He would be where He could keep close watch on them.

The Light of God's Radiant Glory

How many times have you seen the radiant glory of a sunrise or a sunset? These are love paintings into which the Lord pours so much of His love. They are there to be enjoyed by everyone.

The sun brings light that illumines the whole Earth. Unlike a lightbulb, sunlight makes everything beautiful. The sun also brings warmth to the earth. It comes up faithfully every morning and sets faithfully every evening.

At night, God uses His reflective glory of the moon to display the varying degrees of His radiant light of the sun, so that we can see it when it's on the other side of the earth.

The Hebrew word for light that refers to the sunlight in Scripture in Strong's Concordance is "ore" and it means illumination or luminary (in every sense, including lightning, happiness, etc.) clear, day, light (ning), morning, sun. It's the word used in Genesis 1:3 (KJV), *Let there be light.*

The main Greek word for light referring to the sunlight is in the Strong's Concordance, "phos," from an obsol phao meaning to shine, or make manifest by rays, luminous, fire, light.

What if the bright light radiating from the sun is the radiant glory of God? The Bible says that God hides Himself in unapproachable light (1 Timothy 6:16). Sunlight is a very impressive creation. It makes spectacular sunrises and sunsets. It affects our moods, comforts us, and brings life to all of creation. Indeed, all creation needs the life from sunlight. When you begin to realize how awesome that sunlight is, and if it is the radiant glory of God, just imagine how awesome God is!

God's throne, the Garden of Eden and the tree of life used to be on the Earth.

> *And the Lord God planted a garden eastward in Eden; and there He put the man whom He had formed. And out of the ground the Lord God made to grow every tree that is pleasant to the sight, and good for food: the Tree of life also in the midst of the garden, and the tree of knowledge of good and evil. And a river went out of Eden to water the garden: and from thence it was parted, and became into four*

> *heads. The name of the first is Pison: that is it which compasseth the whole land of Havilah, where there is gold; and the gold of that land is good; bdellium and the onyx stone. And the second river is Gihon: the same is that compasseth the whole land of Ethopia. And the name of the third river is named Hiddekel: (the Tigris) that is which goeth toward the east of Assyria. The fourth river is the Euphrates.*
> Genesis 2:8-14

The main river that went out of Eden to water the garden, and became the four rivers that are still there today. God separated the garden and His throne from the land.

Where did He put the Garden of Eden and His Throne? Also, in Genesis 3:24, it says,

> *So He drove out the man; and He placed at the east of the garden of Eden cherubims, and a flaming sword which turned every way, to keep the way of the tree of life.*

Where are the cherebims?

The flaming part that turns every way is the interesting part because when you see pictures of the sun's corona, it is a perfect description. The earth formerly had a corona of water around it. Most of which God used to flood the earth in Noah's time. It could be considered a baptism, as well.

Now, there are always two baptisms–one of water and one of fire (Matthew 3:11). The baptism of fire mentioned in the great tribulation will come from the sun's corona. Scientists theorize that the core of the sun might be cool. Is it possible that heaven could be there?

It sounds like He just put an angel with a flaming sword to the east of the garden to keep man from eating from the Tree of Life. The Hebrew word for "flaming sword" means flames that swirl every way. If you look at a close-up picture of the sun's corona, this is a perfect description. I believe He separated it to inside the sun and put the corona of fire around it. He built a new city there called the New Jerusalem and that city will come back to Earth, and God and man will be reestablished on Earth as it was in the beginning.

I believe people feel weird at first when they hear this revelation, but where is the New Jerusalem hidden? Where is Jesus Who raised in His physical body that still bear the scars from His passion? Where is the Father's throne? They are all spiritual and physical beings. I believe they are in the sun just like the Holy Spirit told me.

> *Other gods are absolutely worthless, for the Lord God is the creator-God, who spread the splendor of the skies! 6. Breath taking brilliance and awe-inspiring majesty radiate through His shining presence. His stunning beauty overwhelms all who come before Him. (Or strength and beauty are in His sanctuary.) Psalms 96:5-6 (TPT)*

> Psalm 36:9 (TPT) says, *The fountain of life flows from you to satisfy me. In Your light of holiness we receive the light of revelation.*

My understanding of this verse is the light surrounding His throne is His radiant glory that illuminates the world.

We had a guest speaker come to our church one time and he was familiar with NASA'S science. He said that NASA has discovered portals that open up from the sun to Earth. Genesis 28:12 talks about Jacob's dream where he saw angels ascending and descending on ladders from heaven to Earth. Could that have been a portal?

> *God's splendor is a tale that is told written in the stars. Space itself speaks his story through the marvels of the heavens. His truth is on tour in the starry vault of the sky, showing*

his skill in creation's craftsmanship. Each day gushes out its message to the next, night by night whispering its knowledge to all-without a sound, without a word, without a voice being heard, yet all the world can hear its echo. Everywhere its message goes out. What a heavenly home God has set for the sun, shining in the superdome of the sky! See how he leaves his celestial chamber each morning, radiant as a bridegroom ready for his wedding, like a day-breaking champion eager to run his course. He rises on one horizon completing his circuit on the other, warming lives and lands with his heat. Psalms 19:1-6 (TPT)

And I John saw the holy city, new Jerusalem, coming down from God out of heaven, prepared as a bride adorned for her husband. Revelation 21:2

I saw no temple therein: for the Lord God Almighty and the Lamb are the temple of it. And the city had no need of the sun, neither of the moon, to shine in it: for the glory of God did lighten it, and the Lamb is the light thereof. Revelation 21:22-23

And, there shall be no night there; and they need no candle, neither the light of sun; for the Lord God giveth them light: and they shall reign forever and ever. Revelation 22:5

The sun shall be no more thy light by day; neither for brightness shall the moon give light unto thee: but the Lord shall be an everlasting light, and thy God thy glory. Isaiah 60:19

And here is one more story for you. My son, Ryan, my nephew, Robbie, and I went out on my boat last summer, and, as I write this, I can still remember the incredible sunset we got to witness on the Chain O' Lakes in Northern Illinois which has some of the most beautiful sunsets. Daily sunrises and sunsets are one of the ways God pours out His "love letters" to us. Though many believe He has His hand on them, they don't realize He is the One behind each sunrise and sunset. So, they miss the awe of knowing it is His radiant glory that causes the beauty we adore.

***

Dear reader, would you like to come to know this awesome God who has been watching over you with a love that is so intense, that you can hardly conceive it? Only a simple prayer is all He is waiting to hear. When you pray this prayer, you will be born again into the Father's family and are in His kingdom forever.

Just pray a prayer like this:

> *Heavenly Father, thank you for sending Your Son, Jesus Christ, into the world to pay the price for my sins. I receive Jesus's death on the cross as my way of salvation. Jesus, please come into my heart and be my Savior. Please fill me with Your Holy Spirit and give me Your strength to walk with You. Amen.*

Next, dear reader, begin to feed your soul daily with His Word, and spend time daily in a quiet place getting to know your glorious and loving Father.

✻✻✻

I was attending an outdoor church one summer. There was a big yard with a nice metal barn. The side of the barn facing the yard was open, and it was raised up above the yard.

The worship team set up in the barn, and the pulpit was in the front facing the yard. We had sunshine every week that summer except for a couple of Sundays that were just slightly misty. What a blessing it was that almost every Sunday lived up to its name!

The yard and barn were at a Farm & Market in Spring Grove, IL. The farmer was a great businessman and a very knowledgeable farmer. He had it set up for people to come and pick their own apples, corn, pumpkins, and strawberries along with many other crops. He was a great blessing to his community. Before the service would begin, this farmer would give a short teaching about how the crops were doing and explain how the crops grow and develop. One of his teachings was about the importance of sunlight to the development of plants and trees.

Later, I pulled up an article from Top Crop Manager by Ross H. Mckenzie The article is called "Understanding the effects of sunlight, temperature, and precipitation." November 22, 2017. The article explained about how the leaves capture the sunlight and the roots pull up the water. The sunlight provides the energy plants needed to convert carbon dioxide and water into carbohydrates and oxygen. The carbohydrates are produced by photosynthesis, and are used for vegetative and reproductive growth, and to increase crop biomass. This can only happen during sunlight.

So, in the same way, the life of God is in the light (just like John 1:4 says) and it flows into all of mankind and nature. The life in our mortal bodies is only temporary, but to get His life for eternity, you must be born again. If you prayed the prayer from earlier, God put His eternal life into your heart. If you die before the Lord comes for His church, your spirit will go directly to heaven and await the great day when Jesus raises our bodies and transforms them into eternal bodies that cannot die.

> *Beloved brothers and sisters, we want you to be quite certain about the truth concerning those who have passed away, so that you won't be overwhelmed with grief life many others who have no hope. For if we believe that Jesus died and rose again, we also believe that God will bring with Jesus those who died while believing in Him. This is the word of the Lord: we who are alive in Him and remain until the Lord appears will be no means have an advantage over those who have already died, for both will rise together. For the Lord himself will appear with the declaration of victory, the shout of an arch angel, and the trumpet blast of God. He will descend from the heavenly realm and command those who are dead in Christ to rise first. Then we who are alive with join them, transported together in clouds to have an encounter with the Lord in the air, and we will be forever joined with*

the Lord. So encourage one another with these truths. 1 Thessalonians 4:13-18 (TPT)

In the beginning, was the Word, And the Word was with God, and the Word was God. The same was in the beginning with God. All things were made by Him; and without Him was not anything made that was made. In Him was life; and the life was the light of men. And the light shineth in darkness; and the darkness comprehended it not. John 1:1-5

Beloved, let us love one another: for love is of God, and everyone that loveth is born of God, and knoweth God. He that loveth not knoweth not God; for God is love. In this was manifested the love of God toward us, because that God sent His only begotten Son into the world, so that we might live through Him. Herein is love, not that we have loved God, but that He loved us, and sent His Son to be the propitiation for our sins. Beloved, if God so loved us, we ought also to love one another. No man hath seen God at any time. If we love one another, God dwelleth in us, and His love is perfected in us. 1 John 4: 7-12

In the first chapter of the Book of John, the Apostle John revealed that God is light. Then later in 1 John 4:7-12, he revealed that God is love. You are first drawn to God through the light of revelation and the more you have experiential knowledge of Him, you get to know Him as great love! This is spiritual light. God's glory goes hand and hand with the sun. The main Hebrew word for glory is "hode" number 1935 Strong's Concordance and means grandeur (i.e., imposing form and appearance).

> *I will praise thee, Oh Lord, among the peoples: I will sing praises unto thee among the nations. 4. For thy mercy is great above the heavens: And thy truth reacheth unto the clouds.* Psalms 108:3-4.

The sun is located above the heavens.

> *Who hast set thy glory above the heavens.* Psalm 8:1b

> *His glory is above the earth and heaven.* Psalm 148:13

> *For with thee is the fountain of life: In thy light shall we see light.* Psalm 36:9

Who covereth thyself with light as a garment:
Who stretchest out the heavens like a curtain:
Psalm 104:2

In Him was life, and the life was the light of men. John 1:4

The Greek word for light here is "phos" and means to shine or make manifest especially by rays. Luminous, fire, light (Strong's Concordance) All of the New Testament scriptures that talk about God's light are this word. The Greek word for moonlight is "phengos" (Strong's Concordance), The bright light of the sun is God's radiant glory.

John 5:35 says John the Baptist was a burning and shining light. The word light here is "lookh'nos" and means a portable lamp or illuminator, candle, light. That's why Jesus said the least in the kingdom of God is greater than John the Baptist (on Earth) because all of us who are born again have the Father, the Son, and the Holy Spirit living in us. We have the great love of the Father in us, and it is shining brightly through us.

Jesus came to reveal His Father's glory. We are made in God's image, so God is like us. He sits on a throne, so we know He has a body, but His is unlimited and far above ours! Scripture tells us of many of our Father's attributes. He also is Spirit and so was the first man,

Adam, until he sinned. His spirit died when he disobeyed and ate of the forbidden fruit. Jesus became a man like us physically, but was not brought into the world through the seed of a man. He was conceived of the Holy Spirit and was free from sin at birth. He had to endure every temptation just like Adam, but He never sinned, so He was the perfect sacrifice required to pay for our sins. He rose from the dead, and then ascended into heaven with the same body. He was transformed into His heavenly body, and yet still bears the scars from the holes on His wrists, feet, and side.

Conclusion: God is in the Sunshine

The sunshine is His radiant glory, and everything we see in the natural is a picture of the spiritual. The love of the Father is a picture of the sunshine. The spiritual is greater than the natural. His love is greater than the sunshine, but similarly displayed in how it beautifies everything.

Nothing can block out the Father's free forgiveness except for the dark clouds of unresolved relational issues. Jesus said if we won't forgive those who trespass against us, He won't forgive us (Matthew 6:15).

The Father's love warms us spiritually and comforts us just like the sunshine. His love is all around, but we must stop and rest in it to enjoy it. I have a boat docked in a wonderful marina with a deck behind it that looks over a nice lake. I love sitting on the pier basking in the warmth of the sun, and enjoying the awesome beauty that God's radiant glory brings on the sky, water, and scenery. Even at night, the Lord made the moon to reflect His radiant glory; it has no light of its own, but reflects the Father's glory and beautifies the nightscapes... especially on the water.

So, the Father's love is the most awesome thing we can experience in this life, and the most important thing about this life. The closer you get to the Father in this life, the closer you will be to Him in eternity. The only problem is you won't know the awesome feeling of His loving presence unless you take the initiative to get into the secret place. Make a place in your home and your schedule so you can get comfortable and sit with Him every morning for at least an hour. Search for soaking music on your internet or social media outlets to quiet your mind. Present yourself to the Father; listen for His still, small voice. Make your requests known to Him, or just sit in silence and wait on Him to fill you with His peace and love. There is no limit to the time we can spend with Him; He is always available. Then, walk with Him through your day, and He will guide you in His ways of love.

You don't have to believe this revelation to get to heaven, but you will miss out on an awesome level of comfort knowing the Father is really is close. Isaiah 66:1a says, *The heaven is my throne, and the earth is my footstool.* A footstool is something very close. It may take some time to believe, but the Father will confirm this

Conclusion: God is in the Sunshine

to you if you ask Him to. He did for me, and I was slow to believe.

Revelation is a gift from God and is so easily missed. In the story Jesus tells of the rich man and Lazarus when the rich man begged Abraham to send Lazarus to warn his brothers about hell, Abraham said, "They have Moses and the prophets. Let them hear them." The rich man said, "No. If someone goes to them from the dead, they will repent." Abraham replied, "If they do not hear Moses and the prophets, neither will they be convinced if someone should rise from the dead." Later, Jesus confirmed this word when He raised His friend Lazarus from the dead and the religious leaders still didn't believe He was from God (Luke 16:14-31).

The Father was hidden in the Son, just as has been hiding in the sun.

> *Philip spoke up, "Lord, show us the Father, and that will be all we need!" Jesus replied, "Philip, I've been with you all this time and you still don't know who I am? How could you ask Me to show you the Father, for anyone who has looked at Me has seen the Father. Don't you believe that the Father is living in Me, and that I am living in the Father? Even My words are not My own, but come from my Father, for He lives in Me and performs His miracles*

> *of power through Me. Believe that I live as one with My Father and that My Father lives as one with Me-or at least, believe because of the miracles I have done.* John 14:8-11 (TPT)

This revelation of heaven being in the sun has greatly enriched my relationship to the Father through Jesus Christ. Every sunset and sunrise are so much more meaningful and strengthen my faith in Him knowing He is always close. The sun is faithful to come up every day and set every night, and is a great picture of the steadfast love and faithfulness of God. So, I remember to thank Him for His steadfast love in the morning and His faithfulness at night.

About the Author

A descendant of some of the Founding Fathers of America. My mother's and my father's families go back to the mid-1600s. They came from England and their descendants fought in every war and at least three of them were signers of the Declaration of Independence.

My father had generational faith in God, and depended on Him for provision and guidance. He was a World War II vet, serving as a medic and a liberator who developed his faith during the war. His faith saved his life and the lives of many people. He also started a concrete contracting business which I started working in at the age of fifteen.

I got married at nineteen and went into business at twenty-four. I enjoyed playing hockey for thirty years. I never thought I would write a book, but God's awesome revelation inspired me to share it.

References

Page 6 – Desmond Dawes

Page 8 – Greek meaning for "strive" ; Hebrew and Greek meaning for "seek"

Page 12 – NASA article about the mystery of the center of the sun

Page 13 – additional research on the corona of the sun

Page 13 – source needed for "volcanic eruptions confirming hell is real"

Page 14 – multiple meanings of "glory"

Page 19 – Strong's Concordance references

Page 20 – Hebrew word for "flaming sword"

Page 22 – Top Crop Manager article (sample citation included)

Page 23 – Strong's Concordance reference

Page 24 – Strong's Concordance reference

Page 24 – meaning of "lookh'nos"

CPSIA information can be obtained
at www.ICGtesting.com
Printed in the USA
LVHW010013120523
746764LV00014B/495